THE CONSTITUTION

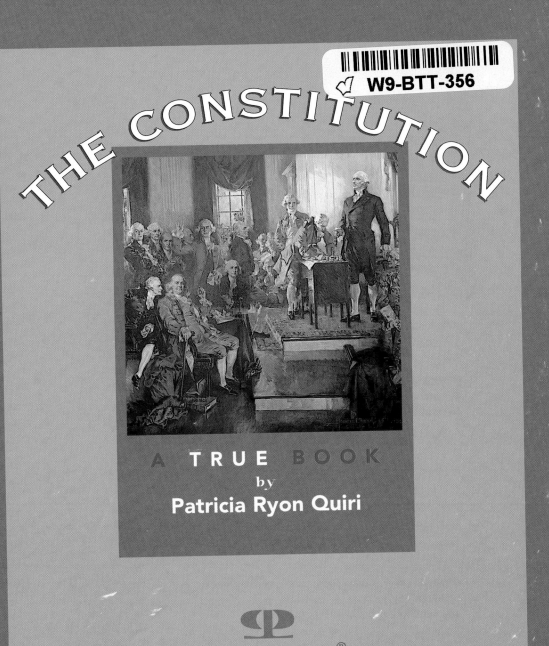

A TRUE BOOK

by

Patricia Ryon Quiri

Children's Press ®
A Division of Grolier Publishing
New York London Hong Kong Sydney
Danbury, Connecticut

Reading Consultant
Linda Cornwell
Learning Resource Consultant
Indiana Department
of Education

Author's Dedication:
For David and Casey Boyer
and in loving memory of
their mother, Susan Boyer,
my Monday mom.

The United States celebrated the two-hundredth anniversary of the Constitution in 1987.

Visit Children's Press on the Internet at:
http://publishing.grolier.com

Library of Congress Cataloging-in-Publication Data

Quiri, Patricia Ryon.
    The Constitution : a true book / by Patricia Ryon Quiri.
        p.   cm. — (A true book)
    Includes bibliographical references (p. 44) and index.
    Summary: Explains why a constitution was needed; describes the convention in Philadelphia in 1787, the Virginia and New Jersey plans, the Great Compromise, and the ratification process.
    ISBN 0-516-20663-X (lib. bdg.)   0-516-26429-X (pbk.)
    1. United States. Constitution—History—Juvenile literature. 2. United States—Politics and government—1783-1789—Juvenile literature. [1. United States. Constitution—History. 2. United States—Politics and government—1783-1789.] I. Title.
E303.Q57 1998   97-48965
973.3—dc21   CIP
                                                                        AC

Contents

The British surrender to George Washington at Yorktown in 1781. Two years later, the American Revolution was officially over.

Independent Nation or States?

The United States won its independence, or freedom, from Great Britain in 1783. At that time, each of the thirteen original states had its own government. The thirteen states were Massachusetts, New Hampshire, Connecticut,

Rhode Island, New Jersey, New York, Maryland, Pennsylvania, Delaware, Virginia, North Carolina, South Carolina, and Georgia.

At first, none of the states wanted a strong central government. Great Britain had ruled them as colonies, and they had not been happy with that. So they set up a government based on rules called the Articles of Confederation. Each state liked having control over

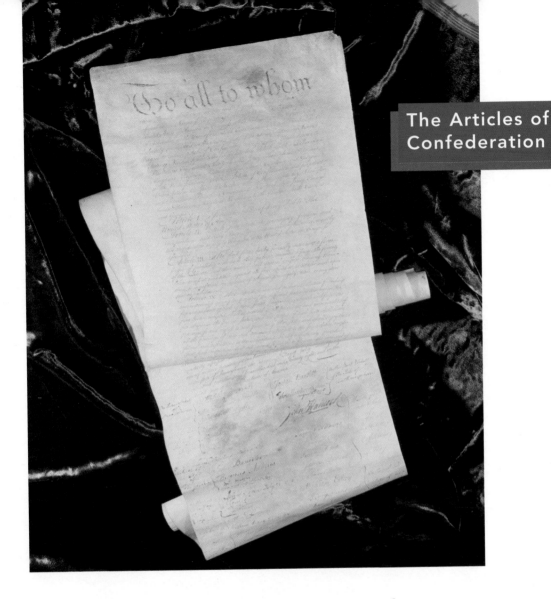

itself. Each state was almost a
separate country. The United
States were not united at all.

In 1797, New York City was already becoming a major business center.

In time, the states realized that their governments were not working well. Maybe they did need a stronger central government. For one thing, the population of the United States was getting bigger and bigger. In 1776, there were 2.5 million people living in the country. In 1787, there were 4 million people. The country was growing.

There were other problems, too. Some states were having

trouble with foreign countries. The central government didn't have the power to help. There were also problems with trade. Again, the central government didn't have the power to help. Farmers in Massachusetts were upset because they could not pay their debts. Soon a farmer named Daniel Shays led hundreds of others in what became known as Shays' Rebellion. The government couldn't help because it had no weapons and no army.

A farmer fights a government supporter during Shays' Rebellion.

All these events made the leaders of the states realize something had to be done. The United States was falling apart. A stronger national government was needed.

The Constitutional Convention

A big meeting, or convention, was called to talk about how the government could work better. Delegates from twelve of the thirteen states met at the State House in Philadelphia on May 14, 1787. Delegates are people appointed to

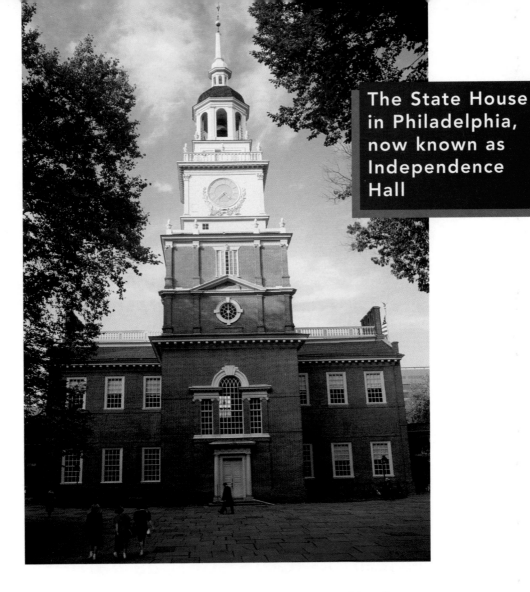

The State House in Philadelphia, now known as Independence Hall

represent a group. All the states except Rhode Island sent delegates.

Some famous delegates to the Constitutional Convention: James Madison (left), Alexander Hamilton (middle), and George Washington (right).

It took many days for the delegates to get to Philadelphia. They traveled by horse, by carriage, or by boat. Well-known American leaders such as James Madison, Alexander Hamilton, George Washington, and Benjamin Franklin came.

Benjamin Franklin, who lived near Philadelphia, didn't come by carriage. He was carried to the meeting in a Chinese sedan chair. He was eighty-one years old and had many aches and pains. Four prisoners carried his sedan chair.

Benjamin Franklin arrives at the Convention in his sedan chair.

John Adams, who eventually became the second president of the United States, did not go to the meeting. He was in England, serving as the U.S. ambassador. An ambassador is a representative from a foreign country. Thomas Jefferson, author of the Declaration of Independence, wasn't there, either. He was in France as the U.S. ambassador. And Patrick Henry, a famous speaker from Virginia, refused to attend. He didn't like the idea of this meeting, saying he "smelled a rat." He was against the idea of a strong central government.

Finally, by May 25, 1787, enough delegates had arrived to begin the meeting. The main purpose of the meeting was to create a plan for a central government. This plan would be called the Constitution. In time, the meeting became known as the Constitutional Convention.

The Constitutional Convention dragged on for sixteen long weeks.

All the delegates agreed to one thing at the beginning of the Constitutional Convention. Someone had to be in charge. George Washington was elected president of the convention.

The fifty-five delegates included the most brilliant men of our country. Their average age was forty-three. These delegates became known as our Founding Fathers. They worked tirelessly to set up a strong central government for the United States of America.

The Virginia Plan and the New Jersey Plan

During the meeting, the heat in Philadelphia was terrible. It was May, but summer came early that year. The men in the State House suffered from the heat even more because they kept all the windows closed. Their discussions at this meeting had to be kept secret.

James Madison, who eventually became the fourth president of the United States, had spent years studying history and government. Madison came up with a plan for the Constitution.

Edmund Randolph, governor of Virginia, presented Madison's plan. The government would be made up of three sections, or branches—

Edmund Randolph, who presented Madison's plan for government

the executive branch, the legislative branch, and the judicial branch.

The executive branch would have a president who was in charge of the govern-ment. He would be president for a certain number of years, called a term.

The legislative branch would have two houses—the House of Representatives and the Senate. They would be called the Congress. These two houses would make the laws. The judicial branch would consist of courts that made sure the laws were obeyed.

This plan for government became known as the Virginia Plan. The smaller states were worried about the Virginia Plan. They thought it would make the government pay more attention to the bigger states. So William Paterson of New Jersey came up with another plan, which became known as the New Jersey Plan. According to this plan, each state would have an equal vote. Congress could control trade and would have the right to tax. The states would have more control than the president.

William Paterson, who presented the New Jersey Plan

James Madison disagreed with this plan, however. Finally, the delegates voted to choose one of the plans. The Virginia Plan won.

The Great Compromise

Under the Virginia Plan, there would be two houses of Congress. These two houses would make laws for the country when it was necessary. One house was the House of Representatives; the other house was the Senate. The smaller states were worried that the bigger states would have more representatives than they had in the houses of Congress.

There were lots of arguments. Not only was the weather outside hot, but the tempers inside were hot, too. Some people threatened to leave. At last, the delegates came to a compromise, or agreement. Ideas from the Virginia Plan and the New Jersey Plan were combined.

During the Constitutional Convention, crowds waited for news outside the State House in Philadelphia.

The new plan became known as the Great Compromise.

According to the Great Compromise, the number of representatives a state could have in the House of Representatives would be based on that state's population. The larger the state, the more representatives it would have. But in the Senate, every state would have two senators, no matter how big or small the state was. This compromise pleased both the large states and small states.

The Constitution

The U.S. government today works the way delegates to the Constitutional Convention planned it. There are two houses of Congress, the Senate and the House of Representatives. Each house meets separately.

The Senate chambers

The chambers of the House of Representatives

The House of Representatives has 438 members. Each member serves a two-year term and then must run for re-election. The Senate has one hundred members, two from each state. Senators serve six-year terms.

New members of the House of Representatives are sworn in.

A committee in the Senate gathers information about a new bill.

After the Great Compromise, the delegates worked on other important matters. They chose one person to be chief executive. They decided to call the chief executive, the "president." Of course, they all had George Washington in mind as president. They decided how long terms of office should be. They also decided how new states could join the Union.

In 1789, George Washington was sworn in as the first U.S. president.

The delegates were careful to create a central government where no one branch had more power than another.

Also, each branch could check the power of the others. The Founding Fathers understood that there might be a need for change in the future, so they made it possible to add amendments, or changes, to the Constitution.

The Founding Fathers also formed the United States Supreme Court. The Supreme Court handled any arguments over the meaning of any part of the Constitution.

Ratifying the Constitution

A committee was formed to write the final copy of the Constitution. It took the committee four days. On September 12, the committee showed the delegates their work. The Constitution began with the words, "We the People . . ." Some liked it, but others started to worry.

The Beginning...

This is the first sentence of the Constitution of the United States:

"**W**e the People of the United States, in Order to form a more perfect Union, establish Justice, insure domestic Tranquillity, provide for the common defense, promote the general Welfare, and secure the Blessings of Liberty to ourselves and our Posterity, do ordain and establish this Constitution for the United States of America."

There was no bill of rights in the Constitution. A bill of rights was needed to protect individual freedoms. (A bill of rights was added eventually in 1791.)

Finally, on September 17, 1787, the Constitution was ready to be signed. Thirty-nine

Signing of the Constitution

of the remaining forty-two delegates signed it.

Now the states had to ratify, or accept, the Constitution. If nine out of thirteen states accepted the Constitution, it would become law.

It took many months for the states to vote. Delaware was the first to ratify the Constitution, on December 7, 1787. The ninth state to ratify the Constitution was New Hampshire on June 21, 1788.

Writings like *The Federalist* convinced the states to ratify the Constitution.

In time, the rest of the states also ratified the Constitution. Rhode Island was the last to do so—in May 1790.

A Government for Years to Come

The fifty-five delegates at the Constitutional Convention worked hard throughout that long, hot summer of 1787. Because of his work, James Madison earned the name Father of the Constitution. He was the only person to make detailed notes of everything that was said and done during the convention.

To this very day, the Constitution provides a framework for American government. No law that goes against the Constitution can be passed.

The fifty-five men who created the Constitution laid the framework for what was to become the greatest and most powerful nation in the world— the United States of America.

Amendments to the Constitution

The first ten amendments, or additions, to the Constitution were ratified in 1791. They are known as the Bill of Rights. The Bill of Rights describes rights that the government cannot take away from the people. These include the right to a trial by jury, the right to freedom of speech, and the right to freedom of religion.

In later years, sixteen more amendments were added to the Constitution. Amendment 13 ended slavery in the United States. Amendment 19 guaranteed women the right to vote. The last amendment, Amendment 26, lowered the voting age to eighteen for all Americans.

Congress of the United States,
begun and held at the City of New-York, on
Wednesday the fourth of March, one thousand seven hundred and eighty nine

The Bill of Rights

To Find Out More

Here are some additional resources to help you learn more about the Constitution:

 **Books**

Bachmann, Steven. **U.S. Constitution for Beginners.** Writers and Readers Publishing, Inc., 1787.

Fritz, Jean. **Shh! We're Writing the Constitution.** G. P. Putnam's Sons, 1987.

Morris, Richard B. **The Constitution.** Lerner Publications Company, 1985.

Quiri, Patricia Ryon. **The Bill of Rights.** Children's Press, 1998.

Constitution Online
http://www.legislate.com/d/ddconst.htm

Read the full text of the Constitution online.

E-mail Addresses for Congress
http://lcweb.loc.gov/gov/global/legislative/email.html

Get your representatives' e-mail addresses by typing in your zip code.

Independence Hall Association
Carpenters' Hall
320 Chestnut Street
Philadelphia, PA 19106
http://www.libertynet.org

The guiding light behind "America's Most Historic Square Mile"

National Archives
700 Pennsylvania Ave., NW
Washington, DC 20408

The original document of the Constitution is on display.

National Museum of American History
Smithsonian Institution
Washington, DC 20560

Exhibitions about early American history

Important Words

ambassador a representative sent from a foreign country

amendment a change in the Constitution

branches parts

chief executive president

colonies groups of people ruled by an out-side power

compromise agreement

convention meeting

delegates representatives

executive concerning the president

independence freedom

judicial concerning courts and judges

legislative law-making

population number of people

ratify accept

term length of time in office

Index

Meet the Author

Patricia Ryon Quiri lives in Palm Harbor, Florida, with her husband Bob and their three sons. She has a B.A. in elementary education from Alfred University in upstate New York. Ms. Quiri currently teaches second grade in the Pinellas County School system. Other books by Ms. Quiri include *The Declaration of Independence*, *The Presidency*, *The Supreme Court*, *The Congress*, and *The Bill of Rights*, as well as a five-book series on American landmarks and symbols. Ms. Quiri has also written several First Books for Franklin Watts.